W9-AVD-088

If You Will, God Will

If You Will, God Will

Prayers and Promises to Release God's Blessings

Harrison House
Tulsa, Oklahoma

Unless otherwise indicated, all Scripture quotations are taken from the King James Version of the Bible.

Scripture quotations marked AMP are taken from The Amplified Bible. Old Testament copyright © 1965, 1987 by Zondervan Corporation. New Testament copyright © 1958, 1987 by the Lockman Foundation. Used by permission.

Scripture quotations marked NIV are taken from the Holy Bible, New International Version®. NIV®. Copyright © 1973, 1978, 1984 by International Bible Society. Used by permission of Zondervan Publishing House. All rights reserved.

Table of Contents

God Will...

Introduction

God's Word is full of wonderful promises for His children. To receive the benefits of these promises, you must know what they are and what allows these promises to come to you.

In the pages to follow, you will find many of these powerful promises and the key to bringing them to you. Take time to read these promises, and ponder their impact in your personal life. Then pray and believe the prayer listed so that you can activate these promises in your life.

God has good plans for you. Start realizing His goodness today.

If you will...

...acknowledge God in all your ways,

God will...

...direct your paths.

Trust in the Lord with all thine heart; and lean not unto thine own understanding. In all thy ways acknowledge him, and he shall direct thy paths.

Proverbs 3:5,6

Father, You know the beginning from the end. You have ordained a plan for my life. That very fact leaves me in such awe! How could I not acknowledge You and seek Your guidance and direction in my every decision?

So now I come to You, the Master Builder, in the name of Jesus. I ask You to show me what You want me to do today. Lead me by Your Word and guide me by Your Holy Spirit, I humbly ask.

I have total confidence in You to direct my actions and lead me in the way I should go. Thank You for this. Amen.

If you will...

...delight in God's law,

God will...

...prosper whatever you do.

But his delight is in the law of the Lord; and in his law doth he meditate day and night. And he shall be like a tree planted by the rivers of water, that bringeth forth his fruit in his season; his leaf also shall not wither; and whatsoever he doeth shall prosper.

Psalm 1:2,3

*I love Your Word; I carry its teachings
with me all the day. As I put
Your Word into my heart, it
produces good fruit and causes me to
prosper in all of my endeavors.*

*Father, in the name of Jesus, I ask
that You cause me to steadily grow
and increase in the knowledge of
Your Word, that You make my way
prosperous and bless me with success
in my endeavor to serve You.*

*Thank You for Your holy written Word.
It is life and light to me. Amen.*

If you will...

...seek God with all of your heart,

God will...

...be found by you.

And ye shall seek me, and find me,

when ye shall search for me with

all your heart.

Jeremiah 29:13

Oh, what a gentle and good God You are! You never force anyone to make a decision. You gently entreat, invite, cajole, and lead.

Throughout Scripture, You invite us to seek You, not as a game of hide and seek, but to let us know You can be found. If we genuinely seek You, we will find You.

I have found You, Father, in all Your power and glory, in all Your sweetness and life, and I love You. I have found You to be true to Your Word in every instance. You have never failed me, nor ever will.

I want all humankind to find You as I have. As I continue to draw near, teach me to know You more fully, more deeply, more richly than ever before. In Jesus' name, I pray. Amen.

If you will...

...pursue righteousness and love,

God will...

...grant you life, prosperity, and honor.

He who pursues righteousness and love finds life, prosperity and honor.

Proverbs 21:21 NIV

Father, I thank You that I have found Jesus, my King. I thank You that I have also found love, for You are love.

I have been made righteous in Your sight because of my faith in the Lord Jesus Christ. Your love was shed abroad in my heart by the Holy Spirit when I believed on Him.

It is my daily quest to grow in the light of righteousness and love and to walk in it.

In finding You, I have found life, prosperity, and honor. Thank You, Lord. Amen.

If you will...

...ask anything according to God's will,

God will...

...hear you and give you what you ask.

And this is the confidence that we have in him, that, if we ask any thing according to his will, he heareth us: and if we know that he hear us, whatsoever we ask, we know that we have the petitions that we desired of him.

1 John 5:14,15

Heavenly Father, if I desire anything from You, I can come before Your throne and ask, knowing You'll give it to me, if it is Your will. The key words are "Your will," and I can find Your will in Your Word.

You never wish to withhold any good thing from me, and You are anxiously waiting for me to ask, so that You can show me Your love and goodness. Thank You for the assurance I have found in knowing that if I ask in Your will, You will hear me and give me what I desire. Amen.

If you will...

...humble yourself in the sight of the Lord,

God will...

...lift you up.

Humble yourselves therefore

under the mighty hand of God,

that he may exalt you in due time.

1 Peter 5:6

*Father, I am reminded that Jesus
humbled Himself by coming to earth in
the likeness of a man and died the
humiliating death of the cross. He is
my Example and Teacher in the ways
that please You. When He humbled
Himself, You highly exalted Him and
gave Him a name above all.*

*I will follow His example and seek to
live, with the Holy Spirit's help,
humbly before the Lord. Show me
quickly if pride threatens to overtake
me. Make me sensitive so I can guard
my mind and heart against the sin of
pride that so offends You. Thank You,
Lord Jesus. Amen.*

If you will...

...be willing to give up the things that are important to you in order to do what is important to God,

God will...

...give all that you gave up back to you in abundance and multiply it.

And he said unto them, Verily I say unto you, There is no man that hath left house, or parents, or brethren, or wife, or children, for the kingdom of God's sake, who shall not receive manifold more in this present time, and in the world to come life everlasting.

Luke 18:29,30

Father, I love You more than life itself. I consider nothing more valuable to me than the truth of the Gospel and the salvation it brings. I freely and willingly go wherever and whenever You may send me. I surrender every area of my life to You, Lord. Use me to further Your kingdom.

You are my joy. My reward is to be fruitful and further Your kingdom's work. My life is full of serving You. Because You see to it that I never lack for anything in this life, I look forward to the one that is to come. Amen.

If you will...

...serve the Lord in righteousness,

God will...

...cause no weapon formed
against you to prosper.

*No weapon that is formed against
thee shall prosper; and every tongue
that shall rise against thee in
judgement thou shalt condemn.
This is the heritage of the servants
of the Lord, and their righteousness
is of me, saith the Lord.*

Isaiah 54:17

Father, I thank You that I am a joint-heir with Jesus Christ and my righteousness is of Him and not from anything I did or could do.

Yet as I seek the Holy Spirit's help to walk in uprightness, no weapon formed against me, no strategy of the enemy, nor sickness, poverty, or destruction shall come near me. You promise to protect me from those who seek me ill will. Those who speak untruthfully about me will be shamed, because I am a servant of the Lord and seek to do His will on earth.

Thank You, God, for causing me to triumph in Christ. Amen.

If you will...

...respect and reverently honor the Lord,

God will...

...give you a satisfied and fulfilled life.

The fear of the Lord tendeth to life:

and he that hath it shall abide

satisfied; he shall not be visited

with evil.

Proverbs 19:23

Father, I do not fear evil, because I have made You my God and Jesus my Lord. I revere You and worship You as my God and my King. You are far more powerful than any enemy that tries to come against me. Your power and goodness are awesome. I praise You and thank You for Your willingness to care for me.
You are a mighty God!

Thank You that because I revere You, You grant me a full and satisfying life free from worry and torment. Amen.

If you will...

...revere God and worship Him,

God will...

...give you healing and joy.

But for you who revere my name,

the sun of righteousness will

rise with healing in its wings.

And you will go out and leap like

calves released from the stall.

Malachi 4:2 NIV

*In Him was life, and the life was the
light of man. Thank You, Father, that
the Son of Righteousness has arisen
and, through His redemptive work,
provided healing for all.*

*Thank You that His healing beams are
shining in me now restoring me to
health, should I need it, and making
me an instrument of healing to others
in need. He is a healing Jesus. Amen.*

If you will...

...listen to the commandments of
the Lord and keep them,

God will...

...keep His covenant of love.

Wherefore it shall come to pass,

if ye hearken to these judgements,

and keep, and do them, that the Lord

thy God shall keep unto thee the

covenant and the mercy which he

sware unto thy fathers.

Deuteronomy 7:12

Dear Father, I thank You that nothing can separate me from Your love. I love You because You first loved me. Your banner over me is love.

I pray that Christ would dwell richly in my heart through faith. May I be rooted and grounded in love. Enable me to begin to grasp and comprehend what is the breadth, and length, and depth, and height of Your love for me. May I know the love of Christ, which surpasses knowledge. Fill me with all Your fullness that I may keep Your covenant of love, in the name of the Lord Jesus Christ. Amen.

If you will...

...love God and serve Him with all your heart and soul,

God will...

...provide everything that you need.

He has given food and provision

to those who reverently and

worshipfully fear Him; He will

remember His covenant forever

and imprint it [on His mind].

Psalm 111:5 AMP

Dear Father, as I serve and obey You, You remember the covenant You made with me, promising to provide all that pertains to life and godliness.

Father, help me to stop worrying about having the things I need. Matthew 6:25-26 tells me not to worry about what I will eat, or drink, or put on, because You provide the birds with food and I am much more valuable to You than birds. You know exactly what I need and You always provide for me in a timely fashion.

Thank You, Father, for supplying all my needs. In Jesus' name I pray, amen.

If you will...

...obey God fully and keep His covenant,

God will...

...make you a treasured possession
in His sight.

Now therefore, if ye will obey

my voice indeed, and keep my

covenant, then ye shall be a

peculiar treasure unto me above all

people: for all the earth is mine.

Exodus 19:5

Dear Father, I thank You that I live under a better covenant, established upon better promises. I endeavor to live by the law of love and fully keep Your covenant.

How honored I am that You would make me Your special treasure and Your protected possession. The extent of Your goodness is hard for me to grasp. You are my exceeding great reward, and I love You. I am so blessed to be Your very own. Amen.

If you will...

...make God's Word the
priority in your life,

God will...

...make you His disciple.

So Jesus said to those Jews who

had believed in Him, If you abide in

My word [hold fast to My teachings

and live in accordance with them],

you are truly My disciples.

John 8:31 AMP

*How I love Your Word; it is my
meditation all day long. I study and
meditate on it day and night so that I
may learn more and more of Your
ways. Your Holy Spirit is my Master
Teacher. I do not learn the truth from
Your Word unless He teaches me.*

*Father, strengthen me to be a doer of
Your Word, I pray. Guide me by Your
Spirit. May I be counted a true disciple
of Jesus. In His name, I pray. Amen.*

If you will...

...pray for the sick,

God will...

...cause them to recover.

And these signs shall follow them that believe; In my name shall they cast out devils; they shall speak with new tongues; they shall take up serpents; and if they drink any deadly thing, it shall not hurt them; they shall lay hands on the sick, and they shall recover.

Mark 16:17,18

Father, because You are the Lord who heals, and because Jesus has elevated the Church to sonship, You have made us partakers of Your healing nature. My natural mind reels at the thought of Your using us in Your mighty healing ministry. Nevertheless, because Your Word says You have, and because Jesus left instructions to do it, by faith and in obedience I will lay hands on the sick.

Thank You, Father. I give You glory and praise. Amen.

If you will...

...forgive others without condemning
or judging,

God will...

...forgive you and neither condemn
nor judge you.

Judge not, and ye shall not

be judged: condemn not, and

ye shall not be condemned:

forgive, and ye shall be forgiven.

Luke 6:37

*There is a Righteous Judge, but I
am not He. How could I judge a thing
correctly, since I only see in part
and know in part. Lord, help me
not to criticize or condemn others,
but to walk in mercy towards them.*

*My responsibility is to pray. So,
dear Father, I pray for the people
that I'm tempted to judge. I ask You to
give them the Spirit of wisdom and
revelation in the knowledge of Christ
Jesus. Enlighten and strengthen them
so that they may see what they need
to see and know what they need to
know for them to be able to stand
in Jesus' name. Amen.*

If you will...

...seek God diligently and persistently
for His blessings,

God will...

...freely give it to you.

*Ask, and it shall be given you;
seek, and ye shall find; knock, and
it shall be opened unto you: for every one
that asketh receiveth; and he that
seeketh findeth; and to him that
knocketh it shall be opened.*

*Or what man is there of you, whom if his
son ask for bread, will he give him a
stone? Or if he ask a fish, will he give
him a serpent? If ye then, being evil,
know how to give good gifts unto your
children, how much more shall your
Father which is in heaven give good
things to them that ask him?*

Matthew 7:7-11

Dear heavenly Father, thank You that You are my very own Father and I am Your very own child. You are good, and everything You do is good. You have given me all things that pertain to life and godliness, and every good and perfect gift comes from You. You never change. Thank You that I can trust You.

Your good and perfect Gift, Christ Jesus, told us we could ask You anything in His name and You would give it to us.

So, Father, in the name of my Lord Jesus Christ, I thank You that You bless my life with many good things.

Amen.

If you will...

...continue in your walk with God,

God will...

...cause you to reign with Christ.

If we suffer, we shall

also reign with him: if we deny him,

he also will deny us.

2 Timothy 2:12

Father, in the name of Jesus, I pray that You help me patiently endure all trials and hardships I experience for the Gospel's sake. Cause me to persevere so that I may realize Your plan for my life now and in the ages to come. Give me boldness and perseverance when I am fearful and tempted to quit.

With the Holy Spirit's help, I will be victorious and know that great joy awaits me. Thank You for this promise, Lord. Amen.

If you will...

...trust in God and keep your mind on Him,

God will...

...keep you in His perfect peace
and be your strength.

Thou wilt keep him in perfect peace,

whose mind is stayed on thee: because

he trusteth in thee. Trust ye in the

Lord for ever: for in the Lord

Jehovah is everlasting strength.

Isaiah 26:3,4

Thank You, Father, that Christ Jesus is my Peace. Through His blood, I can draw close to You. Thank You that He has made a way for me to access Your help.

Father, keeping my mind focused on You helps me trust You more and more. As I trust You, Your peace flows over me and I am able to cast all my cares on You.

I set my thoughts on all that is true, honest, just, pure, lovely, and of a good report. As I focus my thoughts on You, I am in perfect peace. Amen.

If you will...

...call to the Lord for help,

God will...

...heal you.

O Lord my God, I called to you

for help and you healed me.

Psalm 30:2 NIV

Dear Father, Your ear is open to the cry of the righteous. Your desire to heal is still present today, because You have never changed. You wish to heal all illnesses, whether physical, emotional, or spiritual.

Father, I have need of healing. Your Word says that by Jesus' stripes I was healed. (1 Peter 2:24.) Because that is true, I ask You to heal me now. Thank You, Lord. Amen.

If you will...

...worship and obey God,

God will...

...listen to your prayers.

Now we know that God heareth

not sinners: but if any man be a

worshipper of God, and doeth

his will, him he heareth.

John 9:31

Father, I thank You that Jesus was made to be sin for me, so that I may be made the righteousness of God. Through the blood of Jesus, I have the privilege of free access to Your throne.

I come just to worship You today and fellowship in Your presence. I draw close to You and You come close to me in the Secret Place. O Father, I thank You that You are my very own Father and I am Your very own child.

I thank You for Your holy written Word that is forever settled in heaven, and also for Your great plan of redemption.

You've given me Your great and mighty Holy Spirit, who indwells me, helps me, teaches me all things, and leads me into truth.

I worship You, Father, in spirit and truth. You hear my voice and I hear Yours, O Holy Father. I love You. Amen.

If you will...

...believe God can do anything,

God will...

...make all things possible.

Jesus said unto him, If thou canst believe, all things are possible to him that believeth.

Mark 9:23

Father, You are the God with whom all things are possible. You alone hold that power. To access this promise, all I have to do is believe You. You are such a generous and loving God; You long to work on behalf of Your children. Truly, nothing is impossible for You to do. Thank You for telling us this. Amen.

If you will...

...make God your refuge and
dwelling place,

God will...

...protect you from harm.

🌿

Because thou hast made the Lord,

which is my refuge, even the most

High, thy habitation; there shall no

evil befall thee, neither shall any

plague come nigh thy dwelling.

Psalm 91:9,10

Father, You are my refuge in time of trouble. I choose in my heart to make You my dwelling place. In times of trouble, You are there to protect me; in times of peace, You are still there to protect me. I will praise You forever. You are mighty in power and ever faithful to me.

Thank You, Father, that You are always there for me. My life is in Your hands. You are my safe resting place. In the midst of life's struggles, no disaster or harm will befall me. No calamity or violence will come upon my home. Sickness will not approach me and contagion will not enter my rest. Amen.

If you will...

...walk in ways that are pleasing to God,

God will...

...make even your enemies to be
at peace with you.

When a man's ways please the

Lord, he maketh even his enemies

to be at peace with him.

Proverbs 16:7

*Father, not my will but Your will
be done. Help me to live my life in
such a way that it brings honor to You.
As I seek to walk in ways that please
You and bring You glory, show me how
to love my enemies. Show me how to
be a peacemaker, and as I act in the
ways You show me, Your Word
promises that You will cause
peace to reign in my midst.*

*May I walk, live, and conduct myself
in a manner worthy of You. May I
fully please You and desire to
please You in all things. Amen.*

If you will...

...come to Jesus and believe in Him,

God will...

...pour the Holy Spirit out from you as streams of living water to those who thirst.

In the last day, that great day of the feast, Jesus stood and cried, saying, If any man thirst, let him come unto me, and drink. He that believeth on me, as the scripture hath said, out of his belly shall flow rivers of living water. (But this spake he of the Spirit, which they that believe on him should receive....

John 7:37-39

Lord Jesus, I thank You for the gift of the Holy Spirit. I thank You that He lives on the inside of me. Now, Holy Spirit, I give You free course in my life. Live in me and through me to accomplish God's perfect will. Help me to allow you to minister God's grace, mercy, and life to all those I come in contact with. Live big and bold in me to accomplish the ministry that the Lord Jesus desires to do through me so that I may bless others.

Father, because I believe on the Lord Jesus Christ, You empower me with the gift of the Holy Spirit. Just as Jesus said, rivers of Your life flow out of my innermost being. Wherever those rivers flow, everything lives. I give You praise. Amen.

If you will...

...have faith even as small as
a mustard seed,

God will...

...respond mightily to His Word
as we speak it in faith.

*And the Lord said, If ye had faith
as a grain of mustard seed, ye
might say unto this sycamine tree,
Be thou plucked up by the root,
and be thou planted in the sea;
and it should obey you.*

Luke 17:6

*Father, I often feel that my faith is
very small in the light of what I am
facing, but I have confidence in You
and Your Word. Your Word says that
faith comes by hearing and hearing by
the Word of God. As I hear, read,
study, and meditate on Your Word, You
promise that my faith will grow.
Thank You for that, Father.*

*Because action must follow faith, I will
take my faith and use it like David's
small stone and sling it at my giant.
My giant will be rendered powerless.
If You, Lord Jesus, are with me,
nothing can overpower me. Thank You
for that truth, Lord. Amen.*

If you will...

...cleanse yourself as a noble vessel,

God will...

...use you as an instrument for good works.

But in a great house there are not only vessels of gold and of silver, but also of wood and of earth; and some to honour, and some to dishonour. If a man therefore purge himself from these, he shall be a vessel unto honour, sanctified, and meet for the master's use, and prepared unto every good work.

2 Timothy 2:20,21

Father, I yield myself to You as an instrument of righteousness. Cleanse and sanctify me, Lord. Use me as a vessel of honor, I pray.

May I do the works of Jesus and live pleasing in Your sight. You promise to reveal to me if I am ever in error, so I thank You for that. Amen.

If you will...

...delight yourself in God,

God will...

...give you the desires of your heart.

Delight thyself also in the Lord;

and he shall give thee the

desires of thine heart.

Psalm 37:4

Father, I delight in You. You are the joy of my life. When I delight myself in You, Lord, I find that my desires become like Yours. As a result, You promise to give me the desires of my heart as I continue the close fellowship that You treasure. That closeness helps assure that my desires stay the same as Yours and I receive what I ask for.

My heart and Your heart are one. Whatever You prize and desire, I will prize and desire. "Thy will be done" is the cry of my heart. Amen.

If you will...

...love your enemies and do good to them,

God will...

...reward you greatly.

But love ye your enemies, and do good, and lend, hoping for nothing again; and your reward shall be great, and ye shall be the children of the Highest: for he is kind unto the unthankful and to the evil.

Luke 6:35

Father, how can I love my enemies?
How can I do good to them? Within my
own strength it is nearly impossible,
but through Jesus I can do all things,
and because He loved me when I
was unlovable I can love others.

Show me ways to do good to my
enemies, Lord. Give me Your grace to
reach out to them in Your love. May
Your love draw them to You, just as
Your love drew me. As I minister Your
love, may there be increase in Your
kingdom and growth in the body of
Christ. In Jesus' name, I pray. Amen.

If you will...

...live a merciful and truthful life,

God will...

...give you favor and a good name.

Let not mercy and truth forsake

thee: bind them about thy neck;

write them upon the table of thine

heart: so shalt thou find favour

and good understanding in the

sight of God and man.

Proverbs 3:3,4

Father, help me to be merciful and kind. Help me to love with Your love. As I experience Your love and faithfulness firsthand, I am able to give those same blessings to others. You are my Teacher, and I am Your willing student.

As You open doors for me to share Your love with others, please help me to be sensitive and help me be willing to walk through those doors. Use me, Father, to help heal the hurts of others in Jesus' name. Amen.

If you will...

...believe in Jesus and command demons to leave,

God will...

...honor His Word and cause the demons to leave.

And these signs shall follow them that believe; In my name shall they cast out devils....

Mark 16:17

Father, I thank You for power in the name of Jesus. When I invoke His name, it speaks of all He is and all He has done. I thank You that He disarmed all principalities and powers and gave me the authority, through the use of His name, to enforce the devil's defeat.

As Your child, I can use Jesus' authority to wage spiritual warfare against the enemy in order to protect myself, my family, and those to whom I minister. We do not have to suffer at the hands of the devil and his demons. Help me to be spiritually alert and discerning at all times.

Thank You, Father, that the devil has been placed under my feet. Amen.

If you will...

...forgive others,

God will...

...forgive you of your sins.

And when ye stand praying, forgive,

if ye have ought against any: that

your Father also which is in heaven

may forgive you your trespasses.

Mark 11:25

Father, You sent Your Son to die on the cross so that my sins could be forgiven. You don't require that I sacrifice what You did, but only that I be willing to forgive those that wrong me, enabling You to work in both of our lives.

To forgive is never easy, especially someone who has harmed me in a devastating way. When that happens, Father, show me how You love that person and give me the grace to forgive in the power of the Holy Spirit.

I thank You for Your mercy toward me, Father, and for the cleansing blood of Jesus that saves me and keeps me free from sin. Amen.

If you will...

...commit all of your plans to the Lord,

God will...

...cause them to succeed.

Commit thy works unto the Lord, and

thy thoughts shall be established.

Proverbs 16:3

Father, I pray that You will reveal to me Your plan for my life, in the name of Jesus Christ. May I be filled with the knowledge of Your will for my life, so that Your plans will become mine.

In everything I do, I commit my works to You. Cause me to hear Your voice and become sensitive to Your leading. May my life be fruitful in the earth and bring glory to You. Amen.

If you will...

...walk in God's ways and stay close to Him,

God will...

...protect you so that none can stand against you.

For he guards the course of the just and protects the way of his faithful ones.

Proverbs 2:8 NIV

Father, I choose to obey and cling to You as I journey through the life You have given me. As I cling to You, trusting only in You, You drive my enemies from me. Enemies that would threaten to overpower me and crush me are no threat to You, Lord. In fact, You defeated them long ago on the cross for my sake. You are always victorious.

You, Lord Jesus, will cause my enemies to flee before me and make me overcome all obstacles to Your glory.

Teach me to be fully pleasing to You in all that I do. Amen.

If you will...

...humble yourself before God,

God will...

...exalt you.

❧

I tell you, this man went down to his house justified rather than the other: for every one that exalteth himself shall be abased; and he that humbleth himself shall be exalted.

Luke 18:14

Father, I come humbly and reverently before Your throne. I count my life as nothing in the light of Your glory and grace.

You are worthy, O Lord, to receive glory and honor and power. You are the Creator of all things. I was created for Your pleasure. The reason I live is to please You.

My whole joy is to worship You and to serve at Your bidding. Amen.

If you will...

...live a life of righteousness,

God will...

...provide for your needs.

The Lord will not suffer the soul of the righteous to famish: but he casteth away the substance of the wicked.

Proverbs 10:3

Dear Father, once I entered into Your new covenant by Jesus Christ, the Righteous, You became my Provider.

The psalmist said, "I have never seen the righteous forsaken or His seed begging for bread" (Ps. 37:25).

I thank You, Father, that as I walk in the light of the new covenant, I will never suffer hunger or famine. I thank You that You provide every good and pleasant thing for me. Amen.

If you will...

...walk in love toward others,

God will...

...perfect His love in you.

No man hath seen God at any time.

If we love one another, God dwelleth

in us, and his love is perfected in us.

1 John 4:12

Dear Father, cause my love to abound yet more and more and extend to its fullest development, in Jesus' name I pray. The more I walk in love, as You do, the more I grow like You, Lord Jesus, and I am reminded that You dwell in me.

May love be the director of my life. May love be perfected in me, and I be perfected in love. Make me a vessel of Your unconditional love, dear Father. Amen.

If you will...

...reverence the Lord,

God will...

...bless you with long life.

The fear of the Lord prolongeth days: but the years of the wicked shall be shortened.

Proverbs 10:27

I revere You, heavenly Father,
Lord Jesus, and Holy Spirit, with all
of my heart. I learn to revere You
through Your blessed holy Word.

I choose to live my life being grateful
for all You have done for me, by
walking soberly, circumspectly,
and obediently before You.

I thank You that my life is precious
to You and that You have made a way
for me to live a long and fruitful
life upon the earth. Amen.

If you will...

...be pure in heart,

God will...

...reveal Himself to you.

Blessed are the pure in heart:

for they shall see God.

Matthew 5:8

Father, it was not by my works of
righteousness, but rather according
to Your mercy that You saved me by
the washing of my sins and
renewing by the Holy Spirit. You shed
this on me abundantly through
Jesus Christ, my Savior.

By His blood I am made pure. I ask in
the name of Jesus that Your Spirit help
me keep myself pure. May I walk
worthy of You in all things, so that
I may be presented faultless and
unashamed when I someday stand
before You face to face. Amen.

If you will...

...diligently listen to God's Word
and do what it says,

God will...

...defeat your enemies.

*And it shall come to pass, if thou
shalt hearken diligently unto the voice
of the Lord thy God, to observe and
to do all his commandments which I
command thee this day, that...*

*The Lord shall cause thine enemies
that rise up against thee to be
smitten before thy face: they shall
come out against thee one way, and
flee before thee seven ways.*

Deuteronomy 28:1,7

*Father, I thank You for helping me to
listen and heed the voice of Your Spirit
and to be a doer of the Word. As I
believe and obey Your Word, You provide
protection for me from all my enemies.*

*Ephesians 6:12 says that I do not
wrestle against flesh and blood, but
against principalities, against powers,
against the rulers of the darkness of
this world, and against spiritual
wickedness in high places.*

*In obedience to the Word of God,
I resist you, Satan, in the name of
Jesus Christ. I remind you that
Jesus Christ defeated you and your
cohorts by His precious blood, and you
have no lot or part in me.*

*Thank You, dear Father, for the blood of
Jesus Christ, and thank You for making
my enemies flee before me. Amen.*

If you will...

...agree with two or three others in prayer, with faith, believing,

God will...

...cause it to be done.

Again I say unto you, That if two of you shall agree on earth as touching any thing that they shall ask, it shall be done for them of my Father which is in heaven. For where two or three are gathered together in my name, there am I in the midst of them.

Matthew 18:19,20

Dear Father, my friend and I come together in the name of Jesus Christ. We agree in prayer that You will intervene in this situation according to Your Word.

Thank You Father, for the privilege of using His name. When we pray in the name of Jesus, You honor our words just as if Jesus had said them, so we thank You for granting our petition. You are a good Father. Amen.

If you will...

...be merciful toward others,

God will...

...show mercy to you.

Blessed are the merciful: for they

shall obtain mercy.

Matthew 5:7

Father, You are the Father of mercies.
Since I know You, I know mercy.
Because You showed mercy to me,
I can now show mercy to others.

Cause me to become more and more
tenderhearted. Help me to see others
as You see them. May Your compassion
flow through me as a mighty river
that heals, restores, and forgives.
In Jesus' name, I pray. Amen.

If you will...

...be faithful in the small things
God has given you,

God will...

...make you ruler over much.

His lord said unto him, Well done,
thou good and faithful servant:
thou hast been faithful over a
few things, I will make thee ruler
over many things: enter thou
into the joy of thy lord.

Matthew 25:21

Dearest Father, teach me to be faithful to do Your will. I know that each assignment You give me is in preparation for the next one. As I am obedient, I grow spiritually and You can then give me more responsibilities in Your kingdom's work.

Father, in the name of Jesus Christ, cause me to grow and develop in the fruit of faithfulness. Help me to know what it is You would have me do. May I be found faithful in all that You have given into my hand to do, so that You can trust me with any task, large or small. Amen.

If you will...

...honor God with your tithe,

God will...

...open the floodgates of heaven and pour out such a blessing that you won't have room to receive it.

Bring ye all the tithes into the storehouse, that there may be meat in mine house, and prove me now herewith, saith the Lord of hosts, if I will not open you the windows of heaven, and pour you out a blessing, that there shall not be room enough to receive it.

Malachi 3:10

Father, thank You for making this way to bless Your people. I tithe first to show my love for You. I also tithe to provide for those in Your house and for Your work in the earth.

I joyfully and expectantly bring my tithes into my local church. I tithe as unto You. I pray in the name of Jesus Christ, that You will make my gift a blessing to the body of Christ and use it to further the Gospel message.

I thank You for the privilege and the opportunity to give. I thank You that You promise that the windows of blessing will open to me and to all those who tithe. I thank You that the devourer—the thief, the destroyer, the murderer—is rebuked for my sake. You bless me with more than enough to give to every good work.
Thank You, Lord. Amen.

If you will...

...confess your sins to God,

God will...

...be faithful and just to forgive you.

If we confess our sins, he is faithful and just to forgive us our sins, and to cleanse us from all unrighteousness.

1 John 1:9

*Father God, I realize that I have
sinned. I am so thankful that when
I sin, I have Jesus Christ,
the Righteous, as my Advocate.*

*So on the basis of the blood that He
shed for me, I ask You to forgive me of
my sin. Your Word says that if I ask,
You will forgive me of this sin as well
as cleanse me from all unrighteousness,
that is, any other sin I'm unaware I've
committed. I also ask You to strengthen
me and help me to overcome in this area
of my life so that I will not sin again.*

*Father, thank You for forgiving me and
for forgetting my sins forever. Amen.*

If you will...

...hunger and thirst for righteousness,

God will...

...fill you.

Blessed are they which do hunger

and thirst after righteousness:

for they shall be filled.

Matthew 5:6

Father, I thank You that my thirst for righteousness is satisfied first in the New Birth and then even more as I study Your Word and fellowship with You. I thank You that I was made righteous by the blood of Jesus Christ, the Righteous. Because I am now righteous in Your sight, Your ears are open to my prayers.

I pray, heavenly Father, for those in the earth who do still hunger and thirst. Satisfy their hunger with Your Word and quench their thirst with Your Spirit, in Jesus' name. Amen.

If you will...

...come to Jesus with your burdens,

God will...

...give you rest for your soul.

Come unto me, all ye that labour and are heavy laden, and I will give you rest. Take my yoke upon you, and learn of me; for I am meek and lowly in heart: and ye shall find rest unto your souls. For my yoke is easy, and my burden is light.

Matthew 11:28-30

*Father, I come to You and cast all
my cares and burdens upon You.
When my load gets heavy, You are so
faithful to refresh me and give me rest.
All my requests I make known to You.*

*I will learn from You to not let the
cares and trials of this earth burden
me down, and instead, partner with
You to find rest for my soul.*

*I rest in You because You care for me.
It is my privilege to serve You all my
days. I give You praise. Amen.*

If you will...

...love the Lord and call upon Him,

God will...

...rescue you, protect you, deliver you,
honor you, and grant you long life.

*Because he hath set his love upon me,
therefore will I deliver him: I will set
him on high, because he hath known
my name. He shall call upon me, and I
will answer him: I will be with him in
trouble; I will deliver him, and honour
him. With long life will I satisfy him,
and shew him my salvation.*

Psalm 91:14-16

Lord God, I love You because You first loved me. I am Your beloved. You hear me and answer me when I call. You are with me in times of trouble and are faithful to deliver me. You even choose to honor me.

Because I have set my affection upon You, You grant me a long, satisfying life, causing me to overcome in every situation.

Thank You, Father, for loving me. Amen.

If you will...

...believe Jesus works miracles,

God will...

...show you His glory.

Jesus saith unto her, Said I not unto thee, that, if thou wouldest believe, thou shouldest see the glory of God?

John 11:40

Father, I have seen Your power at work. You are the same yesterday, today, and forever. If You worked miracles when You walked the earth, You are willing to work them today. You are the Almighty God, the all-powerful God, and You are good all the time.

I desire to see You work mightily through me, and I will give You all the glory. Let me be a vessel used mightily to further Your kingdom. Show Your love and power to the world through me, I pray, Lord. Amen.

If you will...

...confess your sin to God,

God will...

...grant you mercy.

He that covereth his sins shall not

prosper: but whoso confesseth and

forsaketh them shall have mercy.

Proverbs 28:13

*Father, I need never fear or shrink
from talking to You when I have
sinned. As a child of God, there is
absolutely nothing I can do or say
that You are unwilling to forgive.*

*As Your Holy Spirit convicts me, I will
learn to quickly respond and run to
Your arms of mercy. You are always
faithful and loving to me, and
I can always find mercy and
forgiveness for my contrite heart.
You are good all the time. Amen.*

If you will...

...remain in Jesus,

God will...

...bring forth much fruit in you.

*I am the vine, ye are the branches:
He that abideth in me, and I in him,
the same bringeth forth much fruit:
for without me ye can do nothing.
If a man abide not in me, he is cast
forth as a branch, and is withered;
and men gather them, and cast them
into the fire, and they are burned.
If ye abide in me, and my words
abide in you, ye shall ask what ye
will, and it shall be done unto you.*

John 15:5-7

Father, I will worship You
throughout eternity for grafting me
into the Vine, Christ Jesus.

I grow in Him by feeding on His Words
and meditating on its truth.

Dear Father, I pray that You would
establish me as a fruitful branch
bringing glory and honor to You
by the Lord Jesus Christ. Amen.

If you will...

...call on God and pray to Him,

God will...

...listen to your prayers.

Then shall ye call upon me, and

ye shall go and pray unto me,

and I will hearken unto you.

Jeremiah 29:12

Father, I need no other indication that You have heard me other than Your Word.

You said to call on You and You will listen to me. How blessed we are that You, the Almighty God, Creator of all that is, would take time and interest in us! Because You promise to listen, I will call on You.

Thank You that You hear me, dear Father. Because You hear me, I know I have the answer. You are a prayer-answering God. Amen.

If you will...

...place your hope in the Lord,

God will...

...not allow you to be ashamed.

Yea, let none that wait on thee be

ashamed: let them be ashamed

which transgress without cause.

Psalm 25:3

*Father, I thank You that You protect
me and preserve me as I serve You. In
You alone do I place my hope; if You
don't save me, I won't be saved!*

*I put my trust in You. You will neither
leave me nor forsake me. You are my
God. You are with me even unto the
end of the world. I make my boast
in You, Lord. You are my very present
help in trouble. As I follow Your lead,
I will never be ashamed.*

*I rejoice in Your goodness,
Lord Jesus. Amen.*

If you will...

...listen diligently to the voice of God,

God will...

...bring increase to every area of your life.

❋

And it shall come to pass, if thou shalt hearken diligently unto the voice of the Lord thy God, to observe and to do all his commandments which I command thee this day...

Blessed shall be the fruit of thy body, and the fruit of thy ground, and the fruit of thy cattle, the increase of thy kine, and the flocks of thy sheep.

Deuteronomy 28:1,4

Father, I pray, in Jesus' name, that You would help me to live my life in a wholesome, godly manner, continuing in faith and love with self-restraint. Help my spouse and myself to make a godly home where our children will be brought up in the nurture and admonition of the Lord.

Thank You that our children are blessed and that Your blessing is on all we do because we obey Your Word and listen to Your voice. Amen.

If you will...

...be willing to be persecuted
for the Gospel,

God will...

...reward you greatly in heaven.

*Blessed are they which are persecuted
for righteousness' sake: for theirs is
the kingdom of heaven. Blessed are
ye, when men shall revile you, and
persecute you, and shall say all
manner of evil against you falsely, for
my sake. Rejoice, and be exceeding
glad: for great is your reward in
heaven: for so persecuted they the
prophets which were before you.*

Matthew 5:10-12

Dear Father, the sufferings of this
life are small compared to eternity.
They persecuted my Master, and
I am no above my Master.

All those who live godly lives in
Christ Jesus will suffer persecution.
Since persecution is inevitable,
may I bear it patiently. If I am to enter
into the fellowship of His sufferings,
may I do so for doing well rather than
doing wrong, I pray. Strengthen me,
establish me, settle me, and protect me,
in the name of my Lord Jesus Christ.
Amen.

If you will...

...obey the Word of God,

God will...

...make His love complete in you.

But whoso keepeth his word, in him

verily is the love of God perfected:

hereby know we that we are in him.

1 John 2:5

Father, as I obey Your Word, I will learn how to love You as well as how to love others. The more time I give You to teach me, the more perfected I will become in love.

As I see Your love growing in me, it confirms once again that I am in You and You are working in me—that You love me. What a precious gift Your love is to me! I love You, Lord. Amen.

If you will...

...honor your father and mother,

God will...

...cause you to live long in the land.

Honour thy father and thy mother:

that thy days may be long upon

the land which the

Lord thy God giveth thee.

Exodus 20:12

Dear heavenly Father,
You have made so many avenues of
blessing for we Your people.
What a precious promise—long life.

In this day where parental authority
is undermined, respect is a term
that has lost its true meaning. I pray,
in the name of Jesus, that You teach
me how to restore the dignity of my
home and family. Let me teach others
Your precepts also. I pray that this
generation would learn to prize and
highly value the place parents hold in
developing our future generations.

Show parents the importance of rearing
their children to revere You, dear Lord.
Have mercy on the next generation by
teaching them godly principles to follow.

As we honor our parents and highly
prize them, Your promise is that it will
go well with us and our days will be
long upon the earth. Amen.

If you will...

...revere the Lord and walk in His ways,

God will...

...give blessings and prosperity
to you and your family.

*Blessed is every one that feareth
the Lord; that walketh in his ways.
For thou shalt eat the labour of thine
hands: happy shalt thou be, and it
shall be well with thee. Thy wife shall
be as a fruitful vine by the sides of
thine house: thy children like olive
plants round about thy table.
Behold, that thus shall the man be
blessed that feareth the Lord.*

Psalm 128:1-4

Father, I thank You that when I live according to Your will and Your way, I am blessed in every area of my life. The work of my hands is blessed. I am happy and well and my family is blessed.

You are so good to me; I cannot help but to love, serve, and worship You. Amen.

If you will...

...fight the good fight of faith,

God will...

...award you a crown of righteousness.

🌱

I have fought a good fight, I have finished my course, I have kept the faith: henceforth there is laid up for me a crown of righteousness, which the Lord, the righteous judge, shall give me at that day: and not to me only, but unto all them also that love his appearing.

2 Timothy 4:7,8

Father, I thank You that the fight
I fight is a good one. Jesus has
already triumphed; and so as I battle,
I know I have already won, because
He has already won.

I ask You, in Jesus' name, to strengthen
me that I may stand fast in the liberty
Christ bought for me. May I ever be
faithful to Your Word and be found an
overcomer, a finisher of the course
You have set for my life, that I might
attain the crown of life at Your hand.
Amen.

If you will...

...be kind to the poor,

God will...

...reward you greatly.

He who is kind to the poor lends to

the Lord, and he will reward him

for what he has done.

Proverbs 19:17 NIV

O Father, give me a heart sensitive to the plight and heartache of the poor. Let my heart break as Yours does when I see souls suffering, and let that lead me to action.

Show me how to be most effective in ministering to those who are poor in body, soul, and spirit. Direct my giving, Father, where it will benefit the most. Give me opportunities to bring the poor to the saving knowledge of Jesus Christ and to teach them to prosper through Your laws of giving and receiving.

Even though I ask this only to bring glory to You and to further the cause of the Gospel, You want me to know that my actions and the intent of my heart do not go unnoticed by You. Thank You for opportunities to please You. Amen.

If you will...

...seek the Lord your God with all your heart and soul,

God will...

...be found by you.

But if from thence thou shalt seek the Lord thy God, thou shalt find him, if thou seek him with all thy heart and with all thy soul.

Deuteronomy 4:29

How comforting it is to me to know that when I am seriously looking for You, I can find You, Father. You do not hide from me; You are never too tired or too busy to listen and help me. That You would be so accessible to me is truly humbling. I certainly don't deserve it, but because You love me and are merciful, kind, and patient, You honor me with this privilege, and what a privilege it is!

I'm only just beginning to understand You, so I must take You at Your Word and recall Your faithfulness to me. I seek to know You more and more, Father. Amen.

If you will...

...ask God for wisdom,

God will...

...give it generously.

If any of you lack wisdom, let him

ask of God, that giveth to all men

liberally, and upbraideth not;

and it shall be given him.

James 1:5

Dear Father, I often lack the wisdom
to know the best choice to make.
Thank You that You promise to
generously give me direction, wisdom,
and knowledge. All I have to do is ask.

Because You will never make me feel
foolish or small when I ask, I will
freely run to You when I need help. You
are kind, loving, and generous to me.
You always want the very best for me
and are faithful every time I ask.
I love You, Lord. Amen.

If you will...

...seek first the kingdom of God,

God will...

...add all these things unto you.

But seek ye first the kingdom of God,

and his righteousness; and all these

things shall be added unto you.

Matthew 6:33

*Father, I do not seek my own will,
but only what You would have me do.
I trust You to provide everything
necessary for me to walk out
Your will in my life.*

*I take my eyes off the needs of this
temporary realm and lift them up and
set them on that which is eternal—
reaching the lost and dying of this
world with the Gospel. I will pray for
them, go where You send me, and
say what You want me to say.*

*As You lead me, I will invest my time,
my energy, and my finances into the
work of Your kingdom, knowing that
You will provide for everything I need.
You are so good, Father. Amen.*

If you will...

...give to the poor,

God will...

...give you everything you need.

He that giveth unto the poor shall not lack: but he that hideth his eyes shall have many a curse.

Proverbs 28:27

*Father, I see and give
to those who are poor. If there is more
that I can do, please show me.*

*In every way possible, make me a
blessing to those who are poor.
May I not only share my substance,
but the Gospel with them as well,
in Jesus' name.*

*I thank You that in giving to the poor,
I will never suffer lack. Amen.*

If you will...

...honor the Lord with the firstfruits
of your wealth,

God will...

...bring overflow to your storage places.

Honour the Lord with thy substance,

and with the firstfruits of all thine

increase: so shall thy barns be filled

with plenty, and thy presses shall

burst out with new wine.

Proverbs 3:9,10

Father, I purpose to put You first in all I do, including my financial and material matters.

My tithe is the first check I write when money comes in to me. If I am faithful in honoring You with my tithe, You will supply enough money for offerings too. Father, show me how to use what You give me in ways that please You and accomplish the most good for Your kingdom. Thank You, Father. Amen.

If you will...

...live a life of righteousness,

God will...

...uphold you with His hand.

The steps of a good man are ordered

by the Lord: and he delighteth in his

way. Though he fall, he shall not be

utterly cast down: for the Lord

upholdeth him with his hand.

Psalm 37:23,24

*Father, I thank You that as
I follow You in righteousness and all
godliness, You direct my steps.*

*I am confiding in You. When I miss
a step, You are there to hold me up
with Your loving hand. You are able
to keep me from falling.*

*To the only true God and Savior,
be glory and majesty, dominion
and power, both now and forever.
Amen.*

If you will...

...reverence God and shun evil,

God will...

...bless you with a healthy body.

Be not wise in thine own eyes: fear

the Lord, and depart from evil.

It shall be health to thy navel,

and marrow to thy bones.

Proverbs 3:7,8

*Father, You are the great Physician,
and as I walk in Your will for my life,
You promise me health in my body. And
who knows more than my Creator?
Who better than You to show me what
is healthy for my body, soul, and
spirit? There is no one better than You.*

*I prize Your wisdom above all else.
Make me wise in Your ways, I pray;
open the eyes of my understanding.
May I be filled with Your full, deep,
and clear knowledge, with all
wisdom and understanding.*

*I praise You for Your goodness
and thank You for Your promises,
in Jesus' name. Amen.*

If you will...

...give,

God will...

...give back to you in abundance.

Give, and it shall be given unto you;
good measure, pressed down, and
shaken together, and running over,
shall men give into your bosom.
For with the same measure that
ye mete withal it shall be
measured to you again.

Luke 6:38

Dear Father, I thank You that as I do my part, You will do Yours. Make me a bountiful giver, I pray. Make me sensitive to the genuine needs of others.

May I not only be generous with my substance, but may I also be generous with my time, my love, my strength, and my talent. May my generosity bring glory and praise to You, dear Father. I pray in Jesus' name. Amen.

If you will...

...acknowledge Jesus as the Son of God,

God will...

...live within you.

Whosoever shall confess that

Jesus is the Son of God, God

dwelleth in him, and he in God.

1 John 4:15

*Dear Father, I freely confess that
Jesus is the Son of God.
Through the miracle of the new birth,
You dwell in me and work in me. I am
Yours and You are mine.*

*In the name of Jesus, I pray that
You would teach me to walk in the
light of Your indwelling presence
more and more, so that I may glorify
You in the earth. Amen.*

If you will...

...serve the Lord,

God will...

...bless your food and water and take
sickness from the midst of you.

❈

And ye shall serve the Lord your

God, and he shall bless thy bread,

and thy water; and I will take

sickness away from the midst of thee.

Exodus 23:25

✳

Father, it is my great joy to serve You and to worship You. It is the reason I was created. It is the purpose of my life.

Thank You for blessing my food and my drink and for having taken sickness away from me through the redemptive work of Jesus Christ. Amen.

If you will...

...receive Jesus as your Savior,

God will...

...grant you eternal life.

For God so loved the world, that he gave his only begotten Son, that whosoever believeth in him should not perish, but have everlasting life.

John 3:16

*Father, thank You for loving me
enough to send Jesus to redeem
me from sin.*

*I know that His blood was shed so
that my sins could be forgiven; His
body was broken so that mine could
be made whole. He died so that I
could escape eternal death and be a
partaker of eternal life. Thank You for
sacrificing Your Son, Jesus Christ, for
me. Because I believe this, You assure
me that I have everlasting life.
Thank You, Father. Amen.*

If you will...

...confess with your mouth and believe in your heart that Jesus is Lord,

God will...

...save you.

That if thou shalt confess

with thy mouth the Lord Jesus,

and shalt believe in thine heart

that God hath raised him from

the dead, thou shalt be saved.

Romans 10:9

Father, I believe in my heart that You raised Jesus Christ from the dead. I confess with my mouth that Jesus Christ is my Lord. I give Him total control of my life, and I submit my will to His lordship.

I thank You that, according to Your Word, I am now saved. You are my Father, and Jesus is my Lord. Amen.

Prayer of Salvation

God loves you—no matter who you are, no matter what your past. God loves you so much that He gave His one and only begotten Son for you. The Bible tells us that "...whoever believes in him shall not perish but have eternal life" (John 3:16 NIV). Jesus laid down His life and rose again so that we could spend eternity with Him in heaven and experience His absolute best on earth. If you would like to receive Jesus into your life, say the following prayer out loud and mean it from your heart.

Heavenly Father, I come to You admitting that I am a sinner. Right now, I choose to turn away from sin, and I ask You to cleanse me of all unrighteousness. I believe that Your Son, Jesus, died on the cross to take away my sins. I also believe that He rose again from the dead so that I might be forgiven of my sins and made righteous through faith in Him. I call upon the name of Jesus Christ to be the Savior and Lord of my life. Jesus, I choose to follow You and ask that You fill me with the power of the Holy Spirit. I declare that right now I am a child of God. I am free from sin and full of the righteousness of God. I am saved in Jesus' name. Amen.

If you prayed this prayer to receive Jesus Christ as your Savior for the first time, please contact us on the web at **www.harrisonhouse.com** to receive a free book.

Or you may write to us at
Harrison House
P.O. Box 35035
Tulsa, Oklahoma 74153

Other books by Harrison House

Pray for Our Nation

God's Word for Your Healing

The Pocket Bible on Faith

The Pocket Bible on Protection

The Pocket Bible on Finances

The Pocket Bible on Healing

Additional copies of this book
are available from your local bookstore.

If this book has been a blessing to you
or if you would like to see more of
the Harrison House product line,
please visit us on our website at
www.harrisonhouse.com.

HARRISON HOUSE
Tulsa, Oklahoma 74153

The Harrison House Vision

Proclaiming the truth and the power
Of the Gospel of Jesus Christ
With excellence;

Challenging Christians to
Live victoriously,
Grow spiritually,
Know God intimately.